HOW ECONOMICS WORKS

SAVING MONEY

By Philip Heckman

Lerner Publications Company
Minneapolis

To Nancy, Cass, and Nick for saving me

Special thanks to Theresa Barnett, Jane Jordan Browne, Pat Brueggeman, Alex Dominguez-Johnson, Janet Garkey, Kelly Liddicoat, Mary Mink, Jane Schuchardt, Ryan Schuchardt, Mike Schenk, Susan Tiffany, and Jim Hanson.

Saving Money has been written solely to offer ideas to children about saving money. The author and publisher take no responsibility or liability in the success or failure of the saving opportunities suggested by this book. Children and their parents should contact the appropriate city, state, and federal authorities or other qualified experts for more specific information on banking regulations and taxes.

Lerner Publications Company
A division of Lerner Publishing Group
241 First Avenue North
Minneapolis, MN 55401 U.S.A.

Website address: www.lernerbooks.com

Library of Congress Cataloging-in-Publication Data

Heckman, Philip.
    Saving money / by Philip Heckman.
      p. cm. — (How economics works)
    Includes bibliographical references and index.
    ISBN-13: 978-0-8225-2664-3 (lib. bdg. : alk. paper)
    ISBN-10: 0-8225-2664-6 (lib. bdg. : alk. paper)
    1. Children—Finance, Personal—Juvenile literature. 2. Finance, Personal—
Juvenile literature. 3. Saving and investment—Juvenile literature. I. Title.
II. Series.
    HG179.H3755 2006
    332.6'083—dc22
                                                    2005005658

Manufactured in the United States of America
1 2 3 4 5 6 – DP – 11 10 09 08 07 06

TABLE OF CONTENTS

CHAPTER 1
WHY SAVE?

Good for you. You've taken a step that many adults never do. You've decided to learn about saving money. That gives you a better chance of having the money you need for the future you want.

Simple saving skills work with even the biggest goals in life. Saving money for a music CD is one thing. Saving for a car or vacation or college isn't another thing—it's the same thing.

Saving means waiting. Waiting can be hard. But you can make it easier if you keep your goal in mind. Watching your savings grow until you get what you want can be as much fun as finally spending the money. This book will give you some ideas about how to save for a better future.

THE GOOD NEWS . . .

Saving money means not spending it—yet. Waiting to spend your money might sound like as much fun as having to eat your vegetables. But suppose you have $5, and you spend only $3 today. Then you wait until next week to spend the rest. You still get your full $5's worth of fun. You just spread it out over a longer period. Saving is just another name for future spending.

Here's how saving helps you:

Saving earns money. Banks and credit unions will pay you a fee for being able to use your money. That's right. The money you earn by putting it in a bank or credit union is called interest. An annual or yearly interest rate of 5 percent means that each dollar you save earns a nickel each year. The more dollars you save in a bank or credit union, the more interest you earn.

Saving saves money. Adults sometimes borrow money to buy expensive things, such as cars and houses. Banks and credit unions charge a fee for lending people money. This fee is also called interest. The bigger the loan, the more interest a borrower pays. Interest can add hundreds of dollars or more to the cost of a new car.

VALUE ADDED

"Percent" means "for each hundred." "Percentage" means hundredths of a whole. So 1 percent (often written 1%) equals one part of one hundred. For example, a penny is 1 percent of one dollar.

Most people borrow only when they must. But some borrow too often, to buy things they really don't need right away. Then they have trouble paying back the loan plus interest. If you save instead of borrow to buy the things you need, you won't have to pay the added cost of interest.

Saving helps you borrow. Lenders want to be sure that borrowers will repay their loans. They look for signs that they can trust the people they lend money to. Having a savings account at a bank or credit union helps to show that you're responsible enough to borrow.

Savings can even help you get your first loan. When you go to borrow for the first time, you have no past borrowing record to show that you pay back money on time. But you can use your savings account as a promise. The loan paper you sign says that you'll keep enough money in your savings account at the lender's bank or credit union to repay the loan if you can't pay it back any other way.

Saving feels good. Save for a computer game and feel like you've earned a reward. Save for college and be proud of

VALUE ADDED

Banks and credit unions help people save, invest, and borrow money. A bank's customers and its owners are usually different people. Extra money the bank makes goes to its owners, not its customers. A credit union's customers (called members) are also its owners. Extra money the credit union makes goes to paying members higher interest on their savings and charging lower interest on their loans.

working for your future. Save for emergencies and don't worry about bad luck.

KELLY'S JEWELRY

After high school, Kelly Liddicoat got a job in a jewelry store. She designed original earrings, pendants, and rings. Kelly worked with gold, silver, and gems. She also used titanium. Pieces of this tough metal can only be attached by a special welding machine that can cost $30,000 or more. Kelly could have borrowed money to buy the laser. But her boss let her use his machine while she saved to buy her own.

"I save because I don't like owing people money," she said. "By saving to buy a laser, I avoid paying interest."

For Kelly, saving is just another tool. She said, "It's not that I sit at home and never spend any money. I need to have some fun. But by saving, instead of getting a little something now, I get a lot later."

A savings plan helped Kelly buy this $30,000 laser welding machine for making titanium jewelry.

A girl carrying her piggy bank stands in line to make a savings account deposit. The sooner you start to save your money in a bank or credit union, the sooner it can earn interest and grow.

THE ADVANTAGE OF STARTING YOUNG

Adults have the freedom to do many things that you can't. But you're much better off in one way. You have more of your life ahead of you. Your savings have more time to earn interest and grow. Time is what turns savings into wealth.

Here's an example:

Suppose Alison puts $25 into her savings account each month (that's $300 per year). Kevin does the same. Both earn interest at an annual rate of 5 percent.

The only difference is when they begin. Alison starts on her tenth birthday and keeps saving until the end of her thirty-fourth year. Over twenty-five years, she puts a total of $7,500 into her account. Then for the next twenty-five years, from her thirty-fifth birthday to the end of her fifty-ninth year, she just leaves the money there. All the time, her savings keep earning interest.

Kevin, on the other hand, waits until his thirty-fifth birthday to begin saving. He saves until the end of his fifty-ninth year. Over twenty-five years, he also puts a total of $7,500 in his account.

Who ends up with more money?

Kevin's $7,500 grows to $14,950 in twenty-five years. Alison's $7,500 grows to $52,045 in fifty years. Alison ends up with more than three times as much as Kevin because her $7,500 has twice as long to earn interest.

Time gives you a big advantage, doesn't it? Start saving when you are young, and you'll be way ahead of people who wait. All you need is something to save for and some patience. And the sooner you start, the more money you'll have.

OPENING A SAVINGS ACCOUNT

To start earning interest, you'll want to open a savings account. Ask your parents to take you to their bank or credit union. Get the answers to the following questions:

How much money do I need to open a savings account? This might be as little as $5 or as much as $25.

What interest does the account pay? Savings account interest rates are usually pretty low, around 1 percent to 3 percent. Interest rates can change from time to time.

Do I need to have a certain amount in my account before I earn interest? Some accounts don't start paying interest until the balance (the amount you have in the account) reaches a certain amount. This minimum amount might be as little as $25 or as much as $500. You want an account that has the lowest possible minimum balance—or none at all.

Are there any fees? Some savings accounts have a service charge, usually every month. Some accounts drop the fees if you have a certain minimum balance. Some accounts are free from the start. Avoid paying a fee for saving.

How do I put money into and take money out of my account? Each bank or credit union has its own forms for depositing money (putting it in) or withdrawing money (taking it out). Ask someone to show you how to use them.

How will I know how much money is in my account? With a passbook savings account, a teller who works at the bank or credit union will record all your deposits and

The first page *(upper right)* inside a credit union's savings passbook for young people tells about getting special gifts as the account grows. The second page *(bottom right)* provides spaces to record withdrawals, deposits, interest, and the balance of money in the account.

Welcome to the Zoo Keepers Klub!

The **Zoo Keepers Klub** at Firstel Federal Credit Union is a **fun** way for you to learn about the importance of **saving money**. This book will help you keep track of **deposits**, record **withdrawals**, and watch your **savings grow**. Bring this book to the **credit union** and use the **deposit slips** provided. Write in the amount of money you **add** or **subtract** from your account each time you make a **transaction**. Every time you make a deposit, you'll receive a **prize**! And when your account reaches a **balance** of $250, $500, and $1,000, you will receive a **special gift**!

Date	Withdrawal (-)	Deposit (+)	Interest (+)	Balance (=)	Incentive Earned
					❑ Yes ❑ No Bear Buck $
					❑ Yes ❑ No Bear Buck $
					❑ Yes ❑ No Bear Buck $
					❑ Yes ❑ No Bear Buck $
					❑ Yes ❑ No Bear Buck $

withdrawals in a booklet. This passbook also will show your latest balance. With a statement savings account, you'll receive in the mail a monthly list (statement) of all your deposits and withdrawals. You also might be able to see your account records over the Internet even when your bank or credit union is closed. You will need a secret password to do this.

How do I find the best savings account? If you can, compare savings accounts at a few banks and credit unions. (Remember that each credit union has its own rules for becoming a member. For example, you might have to live in a certain area. Or your parents might have to work for a certain company.)

What will I have to do to open a savings account? You must give some information about yourself. This will include your name and address. You will also need a Social Security number. Next you will sign one or more forms. One or both of your parents will also have to sign. They will be able to make deposits and withdrawals for you, if necessary.

That's all there is to it. With your first account, your savings can start earning money on their own.

BOTTOM LINE Social Security is a U.S. government program to help provide income to the elderly. You can apply for a Social Security number at a local Social Security office or on the Social Security website.

CHAPTER 2
WATCH YOUR SAVINGS GROW

The richest bird in comics is a duck who doesn't like to spend money. Instead, he lets it pile up in an enormous money bin. He loves swimming in the bills and coins. This duck is a great saver, but his money bin is a big mistake.

SAVING, INVESTING—WHAT'S THE DIFFERENCE?

Saving means setting money aside for future spending. Suppose you receive $10 for your birthday. You decide to spend $8 and save the rest. What could you do with that $2 until you're ready to spend it?

You could put the $2 in your money bin. That might be a drawer or piggy bank. It will be safe, but it will always be $2, nothing more. Worse, your $2 will probably buy less in the future. That's because prices usually rise over time, an effect known as inflation. For example, because of inflation, a loaf of bread costs about twice as much as it did twenty-five years ago.

If you're smart, you'll put your $2 to work. You'll find someone who'll pay for the use of your money until you need it. For example, a bank or credit union would like to have your money to make loans to other people. And it would pay you interest for the use of it.

Putting savings to work to earn more money is called investing. Let's take a look at how earned interest affects savings.

Inflation has increased the price of gasoline. In 1956 the price for one gallon of gasoline was $0.26 at this Mobil gas station. In the early twenty-first century, gasoline sells for more than $2 for one gallon.

COMPOUNDING A GOOD THING

Suppose you agree to lend me $100 for one year. I promise to return your $100, of course. But I also promise to give you an extra $8. That's interest on your $100 at a rate of 8 percent.

For me, the $8 is the interest cost for a loan. For you, the $8 is the interest income (earning) from an investment.

Now suppose you lend me $100 for five years at 8 percent interest. You agree to wait the full five years before you get the once-a-year interest earnings. You let me

keep and use the interest I owe you until the end of the five years. I'll pay even more to be able to do that. I'll not only pay you interest on what I borrowed, but after the first year, I'll also pay you interest on the interest I owe you.

Adding each year's interest to my loan in this way is called earning compound interest. With compound interest, your investment and your interest both earn money. You earn more by waiting five years for your interest than you would by taking interest payments each year. In the table *(below),* notice how the interest earned each year becomes part of your investment the following year.

Compound interest growth becomes greater and greater over time. Compound interest makes the world's richest duck look dumb.

COMPOUND INTEREST GROWTH

Year	Investment at start of year	Interest rate during the year	Interest earned plus interest	Investment
1	$100	8%	$100.00 × 0.08 = $8.00	$108.00
2	$108	8%	$108.00 × 0.08 = $8.64	$116.64
3	$116.64	8%	$116.64 × 0.08 = $9.33	$125.97
4	$125.97	8%	$125.97 × 0.08 = $10.08	$136.05
5	$136.05	8%	$136.05 × 0.08 = $10.88	$146.93

INTEREST BY THE YEAR OR BY THE DAY

Almost all investments earn compound interest. The higher the interest rate, the greater the interest growth. An annual interest rate of 6 percent will earn more than twice as much as a rate of 3 percent.

How often interest growth is figured also affects earnings. So far, the examples you've seen show what investments would earn with one interest calculation per year. When a bank or credit union pays compound interest to a savings account more often, the account will yield more earnings. For example, here's what a $500 investment would earn in two years when compound interest is figured more often *(below)*:

HOW MUCH WILL YOU EARN IN TWO YEARS?

5% interest compounded on $500 once each year	$551.25
5% interest compounded on $500 once each month	$552.47
5% interest compounded on $500 once each day	$552.58

In this example, the differences are small. But with bigger investments and more time, daily compound interest earns an investor more than annual compound interest. For example, $10,000 saved for ten years at 6 percent interest compounded daily earns about $312 more than the same amount at 6 percent interest compounded once each year.

THE RULE OF 72

Over many years, interest compounded daily works like magic. The Rule of 72 is a way to estimate how quickly compound interest works. The rule tells you how long it will take to double your investment. Just divide 72 by the interest rate your investment earns. Suppose an investment earns 4 percent interest compounded daily. Because $72 \div 4 = 18$, this investment will double in value in 18 years. But suppose your investment earns 7 percent. Then it will double in a little more than 10 years ($72 \div 7 = 10.2$).

INVESTING REGULARLY

So far in this chapter, we've looked at investing a single amount of money—a lump sum investment. Most people don't have a large lump sum to invest. Instead, they invest small amounts regularly, as Alison and Kevin did in Chapter 1.

Compound interest makes it possible to turn small regular savings into a large investment. Look what compound interest would do to $1 invested each day for fifty years. The table *(right)* shows how much interest the $18,500 total investment would earn over the fifty years at various interest rates.

COMPOUND INTEREST EARNED

Interest rate	Amount earned on $18,500 over fifty years
2%	$13,109
4%	$40,049
6%	$97,843
8%	$226,236
10%	$519,585
12%	$1,204,997

An interest rate of 4 percent more than triples your $18,500 in fifty years. A rate of 12 percent multiplies your money more than sixty-six times! That would make you a millionaire! It's too bad that most savings accounts earn interest at a rate closer to 4 percent than to 12 percent.

CHOICES FOR INVESTORS

So how do you put your savings to work? Banks and credit unions offer many different kinds of savings and investment plans. Different investments have different interest rates. Accounts that allow easy deposits and withdrawals are a good way to store money until you have enough for better-paying investments.

The U.S. government insures some investments, such as savings accounts. That means that if something bad happened to your money in a bank or credit union account, the government would repay up to $100,000 of the savings that you might otherwise have lost.

Most investors have to pay taxes on the interest earnings on most investments. But most kids don't earn enough to have to pay income tax.

Savings Accounts. As a beginner, you'll start with the simplest savings plan. One is the passbook account. Another kind of savings account is the statement account, where you get a report in the mail every month or every three months. The interest rate for both these kinds of accounts is about 1 percent to 2 percent. As you learn and earn, you'll be able to move your money into better-paying investments.

High school students practice making banking deposits and withdrawals at their school in Muskogee, Oklahoma, in 1917.

Money Market Accounts. The accounts sometimes require that you keep a certain amount in your account, a minimum balance, to receive interest on it. And you can only withdraw money a certain number of times each month. Money market accounts will pay from 1 percent to 4 percent interest.

Certificates of Deposit (CDs). You deposit money in a CD for a certain term (period)—from one month to five years. The CD matures (stops earning interest) when the period is over. You can renew the CD for another period, often at the same interest. Generally, the longer the term of the CD, the higher the interest rate, up to about 6 percent. Banks may charge a penalty for withdrawing money from a CD before it matures.

Savings Bonds. You can lend money to the U.S. government for a certain length of time when you buy a bond for as little as $25. These bonds will earn interest of about 3 percent to 6 percent each year for thirty years.

With more money and experience, you can find investments that pay higher rates. Many of these kinds of investments are riskier, however. Their earnings are not guaranteed. That means you could lose money, including some or all of the savings you invested in them. Below are options for investing larger amounts of money. Remember that to invest in bonds, stocks, or funds, you need the help of your parents or grandparents.

Bonds. Buying a bond is like lending money to an organization. It promises to pay back your investment plus interest. Government bonds are loans to U.S., state, and local governments. For most of these, you need to have $1,000 or more to invest and not need the money for months or years. Government bonds can earn between 2 percent and 6 percent. The earnings on many government bonds are tax free.

Corporate bonds are loans to businesses. They usually pay 5 percent to 6 percent interest. Investors have to pay taxes on earnings from corporate bonds.

Stocks. When you buy stocks, you become a part owner of a company. Many stocks pay interest (called dividends), and their prices can change daily. If you sell stocks for more than you paid for them, you make money. But if you have to sell stocks for less than you paid, you lose money. Stock earnings over many years have averaged around 12 percent.

Mutual Funds. Mutual funds are sold by companies that invest in a range of stocks or bonds or a mix of the two. Mutual funds can be a safer way to invest because they

BANK ON IT What percent of U.S. kids between the ages of six and ten own stocks?
A. 3 percent
B. 14 percent
C. 25 percent
(Turn to page 43 for the answer.)

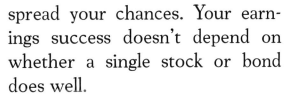

spread your chances. Your earnings success doesn't depend on whether a single stock or bond does well.

Investing sounds hard because there's a lot to earn. To reduce the risk of loss, investors spread their money over many different kinds of investments. They choose a mix of CDs, bonds, and stocks. Spreading out investments in this way is called diversification. A mutual fund can be a good way to diversify your investments.

Many successful investors started young. Talk to your parents about how you can learn together to invest long term. Think about joining an investment club. These are groups of people who get together regularly to study investments. They discuss stocks and bonds and decide as a group how to invest their money. Ask your parents or your teacher to help you find or form a club with classmates or friends.

RYAN'S EDUCATION

Ryan Schuchardt knew that college would cost $48,000. To reach his goal, Ryan ran his own lawn mowing business as a teenager. He saved $8 of every $10 he earned—a total of $15,000. He earned even more by

BANK ON IT Examples of big investment earnings are based on high interest rates and long periods. If your investments earned an average of 10 percent each year, you could almost become a millionaire by investing $1.86 each day for fifty years ($33,945 invested; $966,427 earned).

Ryan displays his college diploma at his graduation. He paid for his college education by saving money and by investing it carefully.

investing his and his parents' savings. "I didn't have to work during college because I saved enough in high school," Ryan said.

Ryan treated investing like a job. He studied companies to find the ones that looked like they would be the most successful. Those companies were the ones he risked his savings on.

Ryan has this advice for you. "A great first step is to save your allowance for something you really want. When you've got enough, blow the money on it. That way you learn how it pays to put off current buying for greater future benefit. Once I started investing, I enjoyed saving. It gave me more money to invest," he said.

SAVINGS GOALS

It helps to organize your savings goals by the time it takes to reach them. Here are some examples:

Goal	Examples
Short term—three months or less	Concert ticket, clothes, gift
Medium term—three months to one year	Bicycle, vacation, drum set
Long term—one year or more	College, house, car

HELP FOR THE HARD PART

How an investment grows depends on three things—the interest rate, the time, and the amount of money you invest.

And where does the money to invest come from? Mostly from money not spent, of course. And as you know, not spending can be hard. For this reason, the next chapter will give you some tricks for successful saving.

BOTTOM LINE Experts estimate that kids see more than twenty thousand TV ads in one year. That's fifty-five messages per day telling you to buy things. On the other hand, how often does someone on TV tell you to save?

CHAPTER 3
SAVING SECRETS

"I wish I started saving when I was young!" This is what most adults say. Their excuse is that when they were young, no one told them how important saving was. You have an advantage because you know this already. Here are some ideas for making the most of your head start.

GET READY, SET, GOAL . . .

Set goals. Which would you rather do—dig a hole or dig a hole and plant a tree in it? The first activity is nothing but work. The second is work with a reward. Put a picture of your savings goal on your bedroom wall. The picture will remind you of the reward you're aiming for.

Make a plan. A savings plan is a written contract with yourself. Putting it on paper makes it real. Telling someone about it makes it harder to quit.

Measure how you're doing. It's encouraging to see your goals getting nearer. Set weekly and monthly savings targets. Record your progress. That way you can see the finish line approaching.

MONEY TALK The tragedy of life doesn't lie in not reaching your goal. The tragedy lies in having no goal to reach.
—Benjamin E. Mays, U.S. educator and minister

KEEP IT UP

Make saving a habit. Giving up today's spending can be hard. But if you do it regularly, soon you won't miss it. Any time you receive money, put a percentage of it in your savings account. When you do this before you spend any of the money, it is called "paying yourself first." After a while, paying yourself first will become a habit that you don't even think about.

Look for work. You can earn money at any age. For most kids, regular chores, such as cleaning their rooms, are unpaid. But all

BOTTOM LINE U.S. families are terrible savers. From each dollar earned, the average U.S. family saves less than three cents. Families in Germany and Japan save double that. And the average French family saves three times as much.

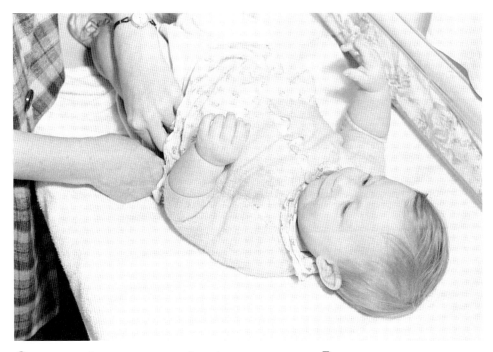

One way to increase your savings is to earn money. Parents may pay you to help them take care of their children.

families have jobs that never seem to get done. Examples are cleaning out closets, the basement, or the garage. Offer to do these jobs for a fee.

With your parents' permission, also ask your neighbors for work. Maybe their dogs need walking or their flower beds need weeding. Maybe their babies need sitting. The more you earn, the more you can save.

MONEY TALK Education costs money, but then so does ignorance.
   —Sir Claus Moser, British economist

Learn special skills. Education is an investment in future income. The more you know, the more jobs you can choose from. On average, better-educated people find better-paying jobs. Look for ways to use education to your advantage. Some parents are willing to pay more for a babysitter who has had Red Cross training for babysitters, for example.

Invest your windfalls. Unexpected money is called a windfall. It's like ripe fruit blown from a tree. Examples are birthday gifts or money you found and can't return. Invest all windfalls for an extra payoff.

BOTTOM LINE
Generally the longer you stay in school, the more you'll earn. On average, finishing high school adds an extra 31 cents to every dollar in your paycheck. Graduating from college adds another 72 cents per dollar on top of that.

Empty your pockets. At the end of the day, put your pocket change in a jar. When the jar is full, put the coins in a savings account to earn interest.

Cut your spending habits. Frequent small expenses add up. Record what you spend each week for things like soda and candy. Figure out what you'd save if you cut back or went without. You could create a windfall of $50 or more each year.

Small expenses add up, and soon you'll find your pockets are empty.

Borrow instead of buy. Got your eye on a music CD or video game? See if you can borrow it from your public library or from a friend.

Buy used instead of new. Dreaming of a bicycle or skateboard? Visit a used sporting goods stores. There you can save half or more of the price of a new item.

Learn about investments. An ordinary savings account is good for starters, but it doesn't earn much. Ask for help in learning about other, better-paying investments. You and your parents might decide to go to the library, bank, or credit union together to get information about stocks, bonds, and mutual funds.

Recruit relatives. Tell your parents and grandparents about your savings goals. They might help by giving you small jobs.

Make it a contest. Make a deal with a buddy to earn and save money together. Compete to see which of you can save the most. Best of all, encourage each other to save and not buy things you don't really need. The buddy system can help you stay on your saving and investing plan.

TRICKS AND TREATS

Saving is like anything difficult. You're always looking for an excuse to get out of it. That's why many adults have their employers put some money from their paychecks directly into their saving accounts. If they don't ever see the money they're saving, they don't spend it.

Here are some other tricks to help you stay on track.

If you find yourself raiding your savings jar for coins to spend, fill the jar with water. Then, when you're tempted to take some change, getting wet will make you think twice.

If your goal is far away, set up some rewards for reaching certain points. Say you need $500 to go to a soccer tournament. Plan to put 5 cents from every dollar you save into a reward fund. Each time you save another $100, spend the $5 in your reward fund on something you enjoy, such as ice cream.

Pat saved $20 a week for fifteen years to buy his dream—a Fat Boy motorcycle.

PAT'S MOTORCYCLE

Pat Brueggeman loves motorcycles. Even though he had driven a motorcycle from the time he was a teenager, he always dreamed of owning the best. He wanted a Harley Davidson Fat Boy. A new one cost about $20,000.

So Pat planned to save $20 a week for as long as it took. He never missed a week. With his savings and interest, it took him more than fifteen years. It wasn't always easy. Sometimes Pat's friends wanted him to spend money from his Harley fund. But Pat never lost sight of his long-term goal. He stuck to it, and he finally got his Fat Boy.

Pat said, "I come from a family of eight kids. That's where I got the discipline. We didn't have a lot. So if you wanted something special, you had to save for it. I always had goals. I was always saving for a bicycle or something.

It might be a sacrifice at times, so you have to reward your-self. Otherwise, what's the point?"

Pat still saves for vacations and other goals. He's encouraging his friends to save with him for a monthlong motorcycle trip out west. They're sure they couldn't do it without him.

DO IT FOR YOURSELF

Think of saving as putting money in a time machine for your future. Your savings goal is your destination. The steps you take along the way should be reasonable for you. Only you can say how much you can give up for tomorrow. That's why you need a plan that's all your own.

Your working life might be fifty years or more. How much of all the money you earn in your lifetime can you save for future spending? How much more can you make it grow by investing? Remember that properly investing $2 each day for fifty years can turn $35,000 into $1 million with hardly any extra work on your part.

Soccer players develop a plan to score goals against each team they play. What plans do you need to reach your savings goal?

CHAPTER 4
YOUR OWN SAVING AND INVESTING PLAN

You've got your money goals. You know how interest makes your savings grow. You're ready to write your saving plan.

START SMALL

It's best to start saving small. The next page shows Tom's quest to buy a camera.

The money Tom saves in this fifteen-week saving quest goes into an account earning 1 percent each year. The chart

TOM'S FIFTEEN-WEEK SAVING QUEST

My goal: **Digital camera**

What it costs: $120

Savings I have already: $15

How much more I need: $105

How much I can save each week: $7

How many weeks: 15

(above) ignores interest earned because the amount saved is small and the time short.

Now let's look at Rachel's five-year saving quest to buy a car. She starts out with $1,500 in a CD that allows her to add $500 at a time. Rachel's CD earns 3 percent each year, compounded monthly. The $75 she saves each month goes into a savings account earning 1 percent each year. Whenever there is more than $500 in this account, she moves $500 of it to her CD so that it earns more. Earnings from interest gave Rachel the $6,000 she needs almost a whole year early!

PLAN TO CHANGE

Think how much you've changed in just the past year. You're probably taller and stronger. (You're certainly smarter about saving and investing for your future.) You don't plan to wear the same clothes from year to year. They wouldn't fit. It's just as silly to think that savings plans you make today will fit forever.

Your savings plan will get you started, guide you, and inspire you to keep going. No plan is so good that it can't change, however. In fact, a plan that won't change is worthless. It can keep you from taking advantage of changes in your life.

MONEY TALK *In preparing for battle I have always found that plans are useless, but planning is indispensible [very important].*
—Dwight D. Eisenhower, general and U.S. president

See if your goals need to change as your income and expenses change. For example, inflation means that prices for the things you need and enjoy will go up in the future. You'll have to earn and save more to be able to buy them at higher future prices.

VALUE ADDED

When you get a job, your paycheck will always be smaller than the amount you've earned. That's because employers must take some U.S. and local government taxes from paychecks.

Your savings and spending plans may need to account for such things as food, clothes, a place to live, and entertainment. But don't forget taxes. They can reduce what you earn by several percentage points. You might have to pay taxes on what you earn from your job and from your investments. Ask an adult to help you figure this out.

You might not have a lot of money to spend or save while you're young. But in a few years, you'll be able to work and earn more. Your savings plans should show that change.

HAVE A MILLION-DOLLAR BIRTHDAY

Want to be a millionaire? You can be, with a plan and the magic of compound interest. Follow it, and $1 million will be your sixtieth birthday present to yourself. (The plan does not include the taxes you'll have to pay.)

Most young savers have limited income. But as they get older, they earn more money and can save more. So the million-dollar birthday plan starts with small weekly savings that increase each year.

The plan has two steps:

Step one. Put money in a savings account each week. (The plan assumes that this savings account earns 1 percent each year.)

Step two. As soon as you have $500 in your savings account, move it to a mutual fund for better earnings. (The plan assumes that the mutual fund earns 9 percent each year, with daily compounding.)

What kind of mutual fund might earn you 9 percent each year? Remember that stocks have earned that and more on average over many years. Other investments also might earn that much. If you choose mutual funds carefully, 9 percent average annual earnings are possible. Your parents can help you find mutual fund information.

Bank N' Save   555554
South Easy Street
Minneapolis, MN   Date 6-13-2005

Pay to the
Order of   MS. SMART SAVER   1,000,000.00

ONE MILLION DOLLARS AND $\frac{00}{100}$

Memo   HAPPY B-DAY!   Barbe Smith

THE STEPS TO $1 MILLION

On your tenth birthday, start putting $1 a week in your savings account. On each birthday after that, increase your weekly savings by $2.

Sometime after your fourteenth birthday, your savings account will reach $500. Use this $500 to buy shares in a mutual fund. Keep putting money into your savings account each week, according to the table. Once each year on your birthday, move all the money in your savings account to the mutual fund.

The million dollar birthday plan will give you $1,040,952 on your sixtieth birthday. You'll have saved $130,000. But that $130,000 will have earned $910,952 in interest. What a nice present to yourself!

As good as that is, you could do even better. For example:

Move money to your mutual fund more often. Many mutual funds allow you to add to your investment whenever you have at least $100. By the time you're twenty-two years old, you'll be saving enough to add the $100 once a month. In this example, shifting money from your savings account to your mutual fund monthly, instead of once each year, would give you $1,068,142 at the age of sixty. That's more than $27,000 extra.

Invest more sooner. You know that the longer compound interest works, the more earnings add up. Suppose you change only one thing in the plan. Increase the weekly amount you save by $1, starting with $2 a week the first year. By saving the extra dollar each week, you could start mutual fund investing one year earlier and you'd end up with $1,118,535. That's more than $50,000 extra!

BOTTOM LINE
Americans keep too much money in low-interest savings accounts. What's the total they lose each year by not investing better?
A. $10 million
B. $100 million
C. $20 billion
(Turn to page 43 for the answer.)

Add windfalls. Any time you have extra income, use it to boost your fund. Include some of your birthday money, pay from odd jobs, or the cash prize for first place in the watermelon-seed-spitting contest.

Keep learning. The Million-Dollar Birthday Plan will get you started. As you learn more about investing, you'll see ways to make the plan better. You'll probably figure out how to invest to reach $1 million even sooner.

WHAT—YOU WORRY?

By now you should be thinking of saving as a journey to a spending goal. Your saving plan is a map. Sometimes you'll find shortcuts, such as windfalls and pay raises. Sometimes you'll find delays and detours, such as car repair bills and job loss. Here are some ideas for beating the obstacles to your savings goals.

Plan for unplanned bad things. No one can say what unusual expenses might appear in your life. You can be sure that some will, though. So why not prepare for them? Experts advise workers to save three- to six-months' income for emergencies. Get in that habit while you're young. Suppose your bike breaks down. It's better to fix it with emergency savings than dipping into your college fund.

Learn about insurance. Some bad events can be very costly. Accidents, for example, can wipe out an emergency fund. That's why people buy insurance. For a fee, insurance companies will pay certain expenses, often including repair bills and doctor's bills. Some

By saving for the unexpected, you'll always be prepared for small emergencies, whether your bike breaks down or you lose your job.

adult workers need life insurance to protect their families against the loss of their income if they die.

But insurance isn't only for older people. Anyone who owns a business, at any age, should have it. And by law, drivers must have auto insurance. This is for car repairs and the medical bills of people involved in a car accident. When you plan to save for your first car, you should also include insurance costs.

VALUE ADDED

Car insurance can cost a lot. In 2003 adult drivers paid an average of $871 each year for car insurance. Teenage drivers, who have the most accidents of any age group, must pay more. Teenage girls might pay 50 percent more than adults. Teenage boys, who have more accidents than girls, might pay twice as much as adults.

The good news is that insurance companies lower rates for young drivers who get good grades. They also lower rates for young drivers who take certain driving courses.

Plan for unplanned good things. Suppose your favorite singer came to town for a concert. You'd hate to miss it. But don't steal from one of your savings plans to buy a ticket. Once you start doing that, it's hard to stop. Instead, build a fun fund. Then you'll be ready for unexpected good times.

ALEXANDRA'S TRIP DOWN UNDER

Alex Dominguez has the travel bug. By the time she was fifteen, she had visited Canada and Mexico. She thought that Australia would be fun to see next. She planned to save at least $1,000 to go there. Her parents would pay the rest.

It was a good thing that Alex also had a savings habit. She had saved $750 for travel in the past. Each year she saved for school clothes too. "Saving is easy," she said, "when you have a goal."

Alex worked at a fast-food restaurant on weekends. She babysat several times a month. Her plan was simple. "I save half of my babysitting money. I also save everything over $100 in my paycheck." Alex's travel fund hit $800 after only a few months. Australia was within reach.

But Alex looked further into the future. She first took out a small loan to buy Christmas presents. She paid it back by having her credit union take money out

Alex Dominguez

of her account every two weeks. Alex knows that her record of repayment will make it easier to borrow more money in the future. A lender will look at her history of responsible saving and borrowing and know she will repay another loan.

ENJOY YOUR FUTURE

The more you save, the better you'll get at it. Learning to plan and to stick to your plan will help you in many ways.

The ability to save is a quality that other people will admire. Friends will be impressed by your belief in yourself. Family members will applaud your self-control. And best of all, you'll feel good about saving for long-term goals.

Savers have less to worry about. They have more to look forward to. With your savings knowledge, you're ready to build a better future for yourself. You don't need anyone to wish you good luck. That's because you're planning on it.

Glossary

account: money kept in a bank or credit union

balance: the total amount of money in a savings account. Balance can also refer to the part of a loan to be repaid.

bond: a loan to a business (corporate bond) or to the government

certificate of deposit (CD): a kind of investment that brings set earnings for a set period. It usually has a penalty for withdrawing money early.

compound interest: money earned on an investment plus interest the investment has already earned

deposit: to put money into an account. A deposit is also the money deposited.

diversification: choosing a mix of investments to reduce the risk of loss in any year

financial institution: a business (bank) or membership organization (credit union) that helps people invest, borrow, and manage their money

inflation: the tendency of the prices of most goods and services to rise over time

interest: a charge to use someone else's money. Investors earn interest. Borrowers pay it.

invest: to put money into savings accounts, CDs, stocks, and bonds to earn interest or to increase in value

investment: a way of earning money by letting a financial institution, business, or government use your savings for a fee

maturity: the end of a certificate of deposit or bond's earning period

money market fund (money market deposit account): a short-term investment that earns more than a basic savings account

mutual fund: a collection of investments that investors can buy shares in. This reduces risk because not all investments will lose money at the same time.

save: to set income aside for future spending

savings account: a kind of investment that earns a small amount of interest and allows easy withdrawal. It is sometimes called a passbook account or a statement account.

savings bond: a kind of government bond

stock: a kind of investment based on part ownership of a business

stock dividends: interest-like payments to investors who buy shares of businesses

tax: a payment to a local, state, or the U.S. government for services such as education and police protection

teller: a person working at the counter in a bank or credit union

wealth: anything you own that has value

windfall: unexpected and unusual income

withdraw: to take money out of an account. Withdrawal refers to the money that is withdrawn.

ANSWERS FOR QUIZ QUESTIONS

Bank on It (p. 21, top): B—14 percent of kids own stock.

Bottom Line (p. 37): C—$20 billion. One expert estimates that the average U.S. family loses $400 each year this way.

SOURCE NOTES

7 Kelly Liddicoat, telephone interview with the author, November 2002.

22 Ryan Schuchardt, telephone interview with the author, November 2002.

25 Benjamin E. Mays, quoted by Marian Wright Edelman in commencement address at Barnard College, *New York Times,* May 16, 1985.

26 Sir Claus Moser, *Daily Telegraph* (London), August 21, 1990.

30 Pat Brueggeman, telephone interview with the author, November 2002.

34 Dwight D. Eisenhower, quoted in Richard Nixon, *Six Crises,* New York: Doubleday, 1969.

41 Alex Dominguez, telephone interview with the author, November 2002.

SELECTED BIBLIOGRAPHY

Bamford, Janet. *Street Wise: A Guide for Teen Investors.* New York: Bloomberg Press, 2000.

Bodnar, Janet. "Money Smart Kids." *Kiplinger.com* www.kiplinger.com/columns/kids/archive.html

——*Raising Money Smart Kids: What They Need to Know about Money and How to Tell Them.* New York: Kiplinger Books, 1999.

Estess, Patricia Schiff. *Kids, Money & Values.* Cincinnati: Betterway Books, 1994.

Gardner, David, and Tom Gardner. *The Motley Fool Investment Guide for Teens: Eight Steps to Having More Money Than Your Parents Ever Dreamed Of.* New York: Fireside, 2002.

Weinstein, Grace W. *Children and Money: A Parents' Guide.* New York: Charterhouse, 1975.

Whitcomb, John E. *Capitate Your Kids: Give Your Kids a Financial Head Start.* New York: Penguin, 2002.

Further Reading

Berry, Joy. *Every Kid's Guide to Making and Managing Money.* New York: Children's Press, 1987.

Godfrey, Neale S. *Neale S. Godfrey's Ultimate Kids' Money Book.* New York: Simon & Schuster, 1998.

Harmon, Hollis Page. *Money Sense for Kids!* Hauppauge, NY: Barron's Educational Series, Inc., 2004.

Honig, Debbie, Gail Karlitz, and Stephen Lewis. *Growing Money: A Complete Investing Guide for Kids.* New York: Price Stern Sloan, 2001.

Mayr, Diane. *The Everything Kids' Money Book: From Saving to Spending to Investing—Learn All about Money!* Avon, MA: Adams Media, 2002.

Websites

AJ's Mall
http://googolplex.cuna.org/00001A/ajsmall/index.html
Click on the various stores in the mall and learn about spending and saving.

Consumer Reports Online for Kids
http://www.zillions.org
This site contains information about products and services including money questions and answers and how to start saving.

5-Spot Clubhouse
http://googolplex.cuna.org/00001A/5spot/index.html
Click on the treasure box and learn interesting facts about money.

Kids' Investment Clubs
http://www.zillions.org/features/invest/invest01.html
This site gives information about the stock market and explains how to set up an investment club for kids.

Learn about Savings Bonds
http://www.publicdebt.treas.gov/sav/savlearn.htm
Learn about savings bonds at this site.

Managing Money: Spending and Saving
http://pbskids.org/itsmylife/money/managing/index.html
Learn about earning, spending, and saving money.

Reach Your Goals by Saving
    http://www.asec.org/tools/ycalcs.htm
    ASEC Tools for Youth provides an interactive savings calculator, a piggy
    bank wrapper, and a savings poster you can download.

Welcome to Planet Orange
    http://www.orangekids.com/home.htm
    Explore the world of money in this interactive site.

Young Investors Network
    http://www.smithbarney.com/yin/ki_home.htm
    This site, sponsored by the investment firm of Smith Barney, presents
    practical information about investing in the stock market.

INDEX

ABOUT THE AUTHOR

Philip Heckman is a playwright and author living in Monona, Wisconsin. He wishes he'd read this book when he was your age. He's kicking himself for not following the million-dollar birthday plan. He'd have more than $900,000 by now.

PHOTO ACKNOWLEDGMENTS

The images in this book are used with the permission of: Bill Hauser pp. 4, 12, 14, 24, 28 (all), 29, 32, 36; © Matthew Fager, p. 7; © age fotostock/SuperStock, pp. 8, 33, 38; Hypnoclips, pp. 11, 21 (both), 23, 25 (both), 26 (bottom), 27 (top), 34, 37; courtesy of TopLine Federal Credit Union, Minneapolis, Minnesota, p. 10 (both); © Minnesota State Historical Society, p. 13; Library of Congress, pp. 19 (LC-DIG-nclc-00663), 26 (LC-USW3-040329-D), 27 (ppmsc 02032); © Rick Schuchardt, p. 22; © Philip Heckman, p. 30; © George Tiedemann/NewSport/ Corbis, p. 31; © Lynsey, p. 41.

Front cover by Bill Hauser. Back cover: Hypnoclips (both).